THE DISAPPEARING TOWN

The Miami University Press Poetry Series
General Editor: James Reiss

The Bridge of Sighs, Steve Orlen
People Live, They Have Lives, Hugh Seidman
This Perfect Life, Kate Knapp Johnson
The Dirt, Nance Van Winckel
Moon Go Away, I Don't Love You No More, Jim Simmerman
Selected Poems: 1965-1995, Hugh Seidman
Neither World, Ralph Angel
Now, Judith Baumel
Long Distance, Aleda Shirley
What Wind Will Do, Debra Bruce
Kisses, Steve Orlen
Brilliant Windows, Larry Kramer
After a Spell, Nance Van Winckel
Kingdom Come, Jim Simmerman
Dark Summer, Molly Bendall
The Disappearing Town, John Drury

THE DISAPPEARING TOWN

John Drury

Miami University Press
Oxford, Ohio

Copyright © 2000 by John Philip Drury
All rights reserved

Library of Congress Cataloging-in-Publication Data

Drury, John Philip, 1950 -
   The disappearing town : poems / by John Drury
     p. cm.
   ISBN 1-881163-31-8 (cloth : alk. paper). – ISBN 1-881163-32-6
(pbk. : alk. paper)
     1. Venice (Italy) - Poetry 2. Maryland - Poetry
   I. Title.
   PS3554.R83D57   2000
   811'.54–dc21   99-40609
                                                                                                    CIP

The paper in this book meets the guidelines
for permanence and durability of the Committee
on Production Guidelines for Book Longevity
of the Council on Library Resources. ∞

Printed in the U.S.A.

9 8 7 6 5 4 3 2 1

Grateful acknowledgment is made to the following publications, in which these poems first appeared:

The Antioch Review: "Soprano"
Columbia: "Lanterns in the Trees"
Denver Quarterly: "Embassy Row"
The Hudson Review: "The Dry Goods Store"
The Iowa Review: "The Fear of Taking Off the Mask"
The Missouri Review: "The Biblical Garden"
The New Republic: "Postmodern Love"
The Paris Review: "The Center of the Block," "Ghazal for My Father," "Ghazal of the Lagoon," "My Father Singing in the Basilica of San Marco," "Summer Jobs," and "Traveling with My Mother"
Ploughshares: "Detasseling Corn"
Poetry: "Decoys" and "Side Panels: Adam and Eve"
Shenandoah: "Descant," "The Disappearing Town," and "Publication of the Bride Sheets"
The Southern Review: "Cuttlefish" and "Sea Nettles"
Western Humanities Review: "Learning Cursive," "March Evening in the Piazzetta," and "Storm on Fishing Bay"

"The Biblical Garden" was reprinted in *The Pushcart Prize XI: Best of the Small Presses* (Pushcart Press, 1986).

I am grateful to the Ingram Merrill Foundation, the Ohio Arts Council, and the Charles Phelps Taft Memorial Fund of the University of Cincinnati for grants that helped me complete this collection.

for Laurie
for Eric and Rebecca
for my mother and my father

Table of Contents

I

Cuttlefish 15
Traveling with My Mother 16
March Evening in the Piazzetta 17
Ghazal of the Lagoon 18
My Father Singing in the Basilica of San Marco . . .19
Ghazal for My Father 20
Sea Nettles 21
Descant 22
The Center of the Block .23
Taking Off the Mask 24
Decoys 25

II

The Disappearing Town .31

III

Summer Jobs 41
Detasseling Corn 44
The Biblical Garden 46
Lanterns in the Trees 50
Embassy Row 52
The Dry Goods Store 54
Soprano 56
Storm on Fishing Bay 59
Side Panels: Adam and Eve 60
Learning Cursive 62
Postmodern Love 63
Publication of the Bride Sheets 64

The deep stream remembers:
Once I was a pond.
What slides away
Provides.

—Theodore Roethke, "Give Way, Ye Gates"

I

Cuttlefish

Beside the rocking dock near the arsenal,
late at night, I hear a man say "Here!"
(but in Italian) "Get it! Get it!" His pal,
much younger with his sneakers and shaved hair,

sloshes a net in the dark basin, lifts
his long pole slowly. As the mesh drips down,
something wiggles and squirms, and the man hefts
the fidgety catch and flips it on the stone

and presses with his pole. Black liquids gush
in spurts and sputters as he pokes it. "Squid?"
I ask the one who caught it. "Cuttlefish."
Tentacles wriggle from a shiny pod.

The creature flutters, plopped on a plastic bag
left open on the stone, emerging like
a flower from its bulb, or a sleek egg
Brueghel might draw, limbs writhing through a crack.

The men continue peering at black waves
through bright reflections—lamplight and bleached poles,
moored boats and stone embankment—for what moves
in pulses, looking for the flick of gills.

The whole canal is inky. Studying
the water, men too agile to get wet
lean out to look for cuttlefish that throng,
drifting like specters, and to drop a net.

Traveling with My Mother

I was sick, more or less, for the whole trip,
and so she got to know the pharmacists
of Venice, claiming it would help to sip
Coca-Colas in cafés, while mists

rolled in like squabbling cats. We squabbled too,
as I threw fits—and luggage—on a bridge,
groaning and arguing as her silence grew.
Which of us could bear the heavier grudge?

Like Proust's *maman*, she stayed in when I prowled
the alleyways at night, making a point
of waiting, lit up in the window, gold
and fractured as mosaics of a saint,

a saint who bitches, patroness of huffs.
We quibbled on the waterbus we rode
along the canyon of pink marble cliffs,
her cane tapping the boat's deck as we stood.

It's hard to translate the unhappiness
of others, even when you learn to spot
a parent's fluttering signals of distress:
all hostile flags at which I had to shoot.

Forgetting our quarrels, she calls the visit "grand."
I like remembering the day she sat
by a bridge, smiling from sky to tree to ground,
letting wind muss her hair, not smoking, quiet.

March Evening in the Piazzetta

Why isn't anybody sitting here
in the one café that's open? There goes
the last family, sneaking out the rear,
miffed at a boy with straws stuck up his nose.

Cats are scurrying by the wall like prowlers,
and I'm the only hold-out. True, a breeze
is shooting through the goalposts of the pillars.
Why is my favorite weather ten degrees

too cool, at least, for anybody else?
People in hoods and down coats make a path
past the café. I wonder why they pause
but don't sit down here. Then I see my breath.

The music's no inducement. A pianist
embellishes the standards that he culls
from a fake book. Flourishing his wine-list,
the waiter lights fat candles in glass bowls.

I won't give up my cold espresso until
somebody comes to sit and hail the waiter,
relieving me. It's late. Where is my bill?
A barge of candles drifts upon the water.

Ghazal of the Lagoon

Morning, on the promenade, there's a break in the light
rain here in the serene republic. I take in the light.

Every walker gets lucky at this gaming table,
where the gondoliers, like croupiers, rake in the light.

Through the glare of a restaurant's window, I see
fish glinting, like spear points that shake in the light.

I could sit on the edge and get wet forever,
all to consider a speed boat's wake in the light.

Furnaces burn. We sweat until we shine, fired up
by the wavy vases glassblowers make in the light.

Row me out, friars, in your *sandolo* on the waves
that glitter like ducats, for God's sake, in the light.

My Father Singing in the Basilica of San Marco

I'll never be as handsome as my father,
singing Vivaldi, when he's seventy-five,
beneath gold domes or strolling by the water.

The choir will go to Harry's Bar together
after the concert. The young tenors grieve:
they'll never be as handsome as my father.

There's one they call my "double." I bet he'd rather
have my dad's full head of hair and never leave
gold domes, humped bridges, and the rising water.

"Why don't you join us? We could use another
voice for the Gloria." But I believe
I'd never hit the high notes like my father.

Gold domes glow like furnaces, the weather
heating up outside when singers move
through the Piazza, thirsty for Scotch and water.

Where's the blown-glass mirror to show each other
what we both fear, what we sing to disprove?
I'll never be as handsome as my father
until our funeral launches cross the water.

GHAZAL FOR MY FATHER

Fishing was our bond. We both hated to be there, weighting
our lines with sinkers, hooking the bait on a hot pier,
  waiting.

We needed Jesus, or at least one of the fishing apostles,
to show us a better spot, where perch and rockfish were
  waiting.

When I dangled my feet in the river, I dreaded the sting
of jellyfish. "Dad, what are we doing here?" "Waiting."

The tackle box creaked open: a tangle of lines and leaders,
floats and rusty hooks, a dull jackknife, our jumbled gear
  waiting.

We forgot to pack lunch. We forgot our hats. Mosquitoes
gaffed us—we forgot the bug repellent, our chests bare,
  waiting.

What did we want, waiting all day for storm clouds to reach us,
waiting for toadfish to snag our lines, waiting for more
  waiting?

When we meet now for dinner, we never talk about fishing.
We order crabs and don't discuss why he left home. We're
  waiting.

Sea Nettles

Ghostly, the nettles floated through a net
staked in the bay, shimmying in to touch
bare legs and backs with slimy tentacles.
"Rub sand on the red spot," my mother said
when I was stung at Chesapeake Beach in August.

Hardly animals at all, the nettles drifted
toward the pebbly shore, scary as mushroom clouds.
Of course they were beautiful—from a distance:
wavering angels poised among the eelgrass.

Lifeguards hauled them out with long-handled nets
and dumped them on the pier. They dried
in the sun, shining like glass paperweights.
But still they stung your foot if you brushed against them,
gobs of Vaseline on the bleached planks.

Washed in and out with the tides, they cruised for food
and sex. No brains, just dangling tangles of nerves
that trailed through the brackish waters of the bay:
clappers of bells whose only ring was pain.

I know they weren't pursuing me like spirits—
except when I dreamed that I was tiny, eyes
open beneath dark waves, treading water
beside a portable cathedral, pillars
that moved, a milky dome that was all mouth.

Descant

At assemblies, on risers
above a band with conga drums
and maracas, I envied the girls
lucky enough, or high-pitched enough,
to sing "dust can"—a melody
soaring over the melody
like a flight of sea birds
raised to a higher power.
But the name had me stumped.
I thought of dust motes
in the auditorium, sifted
through light, dull sediment
settling in a fish tank. I imagined
a chorus above the chorus—
heard on high—sprinkling
confetti from a catwalk.
At home, I scrutinized decanters
and a cloisonné jar
just big enough, my mother said,
to hold her ashes when she died.
It wasn't true, I thought, so I swore
I'd keep a promise
to smuggle the jar, a long time from then,
to the tropics, hire a pilot
to sweep above the islands, and release the dust
in a drizzle through infinite skies,
gliding home
in the head winds over the Caribbean.

The Center of the Block

Hudsons and Studebakers ruled the streets,
a crossing guard and teenagers the pavement
when I was eight. But that was an improvement
on indoors, a domain of grunts and threats.

One way out went up, skyward, on steep roofs
where we clattered on corrugated tin
or gripped crumbling shingles and stared at the sun,
until a call to scat down cuffed our laughs.

We shimmied down the shaky drainpipes, hopped
on the slick decks of sailboats on their trailers
and skulked away, out of the range of callers
to the center of the block, where we escaped.

The boundaries dwindled to a row of wickets
and a wire fence twisted and bent back, pulled
up from a channel clawed in earth. We crawled
underneath and squeezed through, dirt in our pockets.

The bushes, vines, underbrush, limbs, and creepers
were ours, a lodge for the diminutive,
and summer passed in coolness through the cove,
until we rose, pants brushed off, checking our zippers.

Taking Off the Mask

A fear of taking off the mask
Paralyzes the burned boy, fitted in tights
With openings for eyes, ears, mouth,
And charred fingertips. After taunting him
His classmates try to coax him—
Go on. It's OK. We won't laugh.
And if he peels it off,
No, they don't laugh, they are terrified.
Another child, unmarked, could feel
Just as afraid of being seen,
Of opening to a crowd, his face
As changeable as mercury.
It burns and shames him
Because he has no right to such pain,
Having never suffered, having never been touched—
Like a boy he read about,
Diving for coins
In a swimming hole at the edge
Of Nagasaki, only to surface
With his friends gone and the whole world leveled.
Like that. But for no good reason.

Decoys

1.

Lure makers start with deer hair, hackles,
herls from a plume or a swatch of fabric
to craft an illusion with a barbed hook.

The trout may think it sees a minnow,
or a hopper on the water, or a mayfly.
Deadly ambiguity. But ducks are drawn by kinship.

A waterman gouges an eye, curves a bill,
carves pine to feathers as his father taught him.
It hardly matters how crude the likeness, if it floats.

Sometimes a live duck is trapped and leashed:
it paddles, and rises to flap its wings, and calls
in its usual quack, both warning and welcome.

Sometimes a dipper is set with the rest:
a dead bird staked as if feeding underwater,
its tail lifted up in the wind.

Hunters lie in a blind, or squat to deal
poker with shells for chips, except for the guide,
squinting until specks appear. Ready. Now.

2.

In a paneled room, a mallard spreads its wings
but never moves: the glass eyes catch
the hall light. A child, surrounded by waterfowl

and a squirrel turned upside down, begs
for another guest room and old stuffed animals,
without claws or beaks, to hug until he falls asleep.

When he wakes, the car pulls off on a dirt road,
hobbling into ruts until the landing. A posse
cracks open shotguns. He's never seen

such long binoculars. Then the boat pushes off,
oars creak, water plashes as the shore recedes.
Half way out a flock passes over, but no one shoots:

not time yet. Stragglers follow a long formation
under films of clouds. Wind blows after them,
drawn like wake behind them: the faintest wind.

And then they reach the blind, a bale
of rickety sticks with the roof blown off, dark as smudges
on the water. And the decoys start to drift.

3.

So a boy who couldn't hit a tin can
learns the trick of double triggers: if one round misses,
the other won't. Shotguns spray so far,

a duck might think it, if he thought,
hail rising from earth. But now it drags him down,
now it swells like black eggs in his belly.

In the distance, the boy sees a canvasback
drop limp before he hears a rumble of shots
from the other shore, a mile away.

And black clouds rise from fortresses of driftwood.
And tonight, they say, they will roast the dark meat.
And if you bite birdshot, it brings good luck.

But what luck guides him into sleep, when all he hears
are gunshots echoing? Grasping a hand,
he's slipped a charm for his pocket: a webbed foot

softened overnight in vinegar. A paddle
he can twist between his fingers while he waits—
and wishes the sky would darken above the marsh.

4.

Out skipping oyster shells, he comes to a shanty:
abandoned, its pier half washed away, a pile
of crabpots and decapitated decoys by the shore.

Too much handling, too much twisting on a tether
has broken their necks. He stares at the fragments
of cracked pine, bleached on top but dark underneath,

losing their wings as paint flakes. On the water's edge
living is so unsure: you drift with the tides
from mud flats to estuaries, drawn by the wind

as ducks are drawn like metal to a magnet, the terrain
enlarging as they sweep below, ready to pitch in shallows.
He too has dreamed of flight. Not a shooting gallery—

dented tin that flips back when it's hit,
resurfacing in a loop. And not the rush of *Open fire,*
wings scattering in the air. Another flight.

Circling these leavings, he kneels to pick up
scraps of discarded wood—a head, a body—
and pieces together one likeness that is whole.

II

The Disappearing Town

Over the palings of the backyard fence,
over white paint gumming my fingers, over pointed stakes,
over stacked planks with orange nails bent sideways,
past the tilting shed, past the overgrown brambles of the
   rock garden,
through boxwood in a tunnel, under tightly snarled branches
with leaves as tiny as doll house saucers, yellow where dogs
   had peed,
down newly tarred streets, glistening and steaming, the
   gravel wedging in my sneakers,
through the riverside park with its marble torch and high-
   spurting fountain,
past the ship's elevator disguised as a smoke stack,
past Long Wharf, where the presidential yacht, swabbed
   down in the sunlight, still docked,
past fuel tanks, boatyards, crabhouses, canneries,
I ran from my father and was never winded.

> Where did he go?
> Had the bank set off
> an alarm, just in case
> his cash drawer, locked
> in the cold vault,
> lay empty? Was the car
> still missing
> from our one-way street?

My mother was down on her knees:
a trowel in her hand, black dirt on her hands,
poring over her apron as though it were a newspaper.

The lowest branches moved, crape myrtle leaves twirled like
   a carnival ride,
but she could not be disturbed. On her bedroom door,
a hotel sign trembled on its frayed string.
I wanted to knock, I wanted to twist the knob until it gave,
I wanted to lock up the piano, propped by the pier glass:
scratched black crate I had to practice on,
under the painting of a churned-up sea, where a lifeboat,
manned by conquistadors, bucked for land through sharp
   rocks and breakers.

   But what did I know
   of water? A block away,
   the river flowed. What
   did I know? My father
   couldn't show me
   or even tell me.
   What I knew, I felt.
   I wasn't teachable.

Everything swung in motion from a whirligig, blending in
   horizontal bands
until it creaked and clanked, slowing down, wobbly and
   dizzying.
A face returned, the neighborhood arranged itself again.
Standing, I felt my first drunkenness,
wavering through the slime of Seckel pears, dodging stray
   bees and stamping up
to the back porch, its cold apples and cases of pop.
When noon struck, the churchbells went berserk and the
   dogs joined in.

When a storm struck, our house pitched like a boat,
    unmoored,
the phone lines down, snaking through the flood.
The attic was dark, then a shade flared, boards glowed
    like hot metal—then darkness.

        Daytime, I sat on a piling
        for the summer regatta.
        Hydroplanes veered
        like a comet, roared
        on the Fourth of July
        and lit up the water.
        Blue water,
        Nanticokes called
        our river, but often
        it was gray: a vast
        unanswering gray
        that could swallow up anything.

I looked at the harbor, its oily water, its rainbows:
a ladder went down, the warped rungs wavering underwater;
an old door rotted on the park grass, its china knob chipped
    and loose.
But there was no descent in the flat land of marshes,
unless I crawled beneath a porch, its lattice-light and cool
    vault of dirt,
unless I dug for treasure I'd made up on a map.

So much missed, a dominion within my reach:
never skating on the marbly ice by the jailhouse,
never rafting down the river, never sailing on the bay,

never climbing the sawdust in the lumberyard, a tan heap
    higher than a house
where king-of-the-mountain could drown you in pine,
never learning to swim, only a dog paddle, only the dead
    man's float,
afraid of treading water, afraid of touching jellyfish,
afraid of opening my eyes in the river,
the river of coded flags and the ringing, swaying churches
    of the buoys.

> It was our lowly Choptank,
> broadly flowing—
> broad as a sunlit plaza,
> cobbles still gray,
> broad as a flock of geese
> in the overcast sky,
> broad as a barrier island—
> under a sandy cliff
> a few feet high,
> where children
> clawed for arrowheads
> and wandered
> into pine woods,
> where they took off
> their clothes
> on soft needles.

Given the chance, they stripped anywhere:
under a circus tent of leaves, under damp sheets on a
    clothesline,
under the tarp of a sailboat, cradled on its trailer,

unzipping their pants and stowing them, learning sleek
    varnish
and the plush of cushions and the biting edge of cross-
    boards on the bottom.

    And they climbed up
    over shingles and tin
    and down the magnolia,
    leaves leathery
    as shoe tongues.
    And the wind burst
    through a house half built,
    bare struts, the wind
    on bare skin. And one day
    they caught a fish
    with a clear eye
    they thought was a diamond,
    a brewery's promotion
    on the radio:
    Diamond Jim! We got him!
    But when they dumped
    their catch in a wagon
    and tugged it home,
    their only reward was
    "No, it's a blowfish."

I wasn't growing up but apart, like a pier leaning farther
    from shore,
its planks a broken comb, hunched in the middle
like a bristling cat, unaccompanied, apart.
When I went to the bank before he left, my father's hands,

dirty from the cash he handled, reached from his cage.
My mother's hands, ghost white, dusted with flour,
   shooed me
out the screen door, past the wringer of the washing
   machine.

   Love was something else:
   a girl in my class
   who kicked her penny loafers
   to the blackboard.
   Towed by a cabin cruiser
   piloted by her father,
   I lost my grip
   on the life-belt, flailed
   at the water, choked on salt.
   The girl held on
   and watched me
   tangled in waves,
   the boat idling, circling
   in the distance,
   gray sky and water,
   the middle of the river.
   "Stand up," she called,
   "it's shallow, you can walk."
   And when I tried,
   my feet touched bottom.

Years later, the girl who had talked me back from panic
drowned when her sailboat capsized in a squall.
As her mate crawled landward, she bobbed in a life vest.
Nothing for a week, then beached by the puny waves

where green tires, traps to catch sand,
held on to the shore that still, even now, recedes.
No one would know that face, rubbed out, a likeness of
    the river, no one.

> Moving away, towing
> a rented trailer,
> crossing the low bridge
> named for a relative,
> once the governor,
> white caps gleaming
> like helmets in a cornfield,
> my mother made promises.
> And the bridge
> went on and on—
> past blacks
> leaning out to fish,
> over grates, tires whining,
> beyond the water tower
> sinking
> with the town's name
> on its side.

I could ask my mother: *Why did you hold a glass to the
    motel's wall?*
I could ask my father: *Where were you hurrying in the
    middle of the night?*

But they packed in secrecy, changing the subject, not
    leaving notes,
rushing to distant cities where they holed up, apart,

over flashing lights, over fruit-stall awnings
until solitude routed them, as it roots out everyone afraid
   of drowning,
afraid of whirlpools, afraid the water will never begin to
   revolve.
The disappearing town. Let the river take it.

III

Summer Jobs

1. Motor Lodge

"So this is it, experience," I thought,
lugging tin buckets from the ice machines
to rooms of real adults with cigarettes,
mixed drinks in plastic cups, and proffered coins.

I reached out for their blessings, but the tips
were nothing next to rumpled, unmade beds
at four in the afternoon, women in slips
and men in t-shirts while the TV played.

Down in the laundry room, I counted sheets,
stunned by the musk that vanished in the wash,
and balled up soggy towels that down the chutes
exploded in bins. Before the evening rush,

avid and timid for what I glimpsed at work,
I left, hanging my gold vest on a hook.

2. Drive-In Restaurant

The tipping was so bad, I came in early
to wipe hard mustard off the microphones
and lit-up menus in the parking lot.
Each time I took an order, I forgot
something they had to have: two extra spoons,
a moistened napkin, hot sauce for the chili.

I was the oddball who didn't speak Persian,
who hadn't flown the ocean, who hadn't fought
battles with chains and switchblades in the slums,
who couldn't balance trays upon his palms,
who hadn't lost a parent, who hadn't built
wire traps to capture animals for rations.

After the midnight movie crowd peeled out,
I picked up trash from each damned parking spot.

3. Apartment Complex

"John Slow" they called me, when I worked outdoors,
hauling lawn mowers up a steep incline,
heaving "sod clods" off trucks, buffing the floors
of vacated apartments. By design,
I didn't hurry undertaking tasks
like weeding the rock garden, scrubbing walls
where mildew blackened, piling up old desks.
It all seeped deeper in my overalls.

They said I looked like Rudolf Valentino
because of my slicked-back hair. Because I was silent?
Sweeping the stairs, I stopped when a piano
echoed above the cool well where dust gathered.
Loafing, the boss said, is your only talent—
while the sod we planted on the hard earth withered.

Detasseling Corn

I'm here because I needed work, two acres worth,
where damp earth slows me in the morning

and spiders drop like parachutes
if I brush the leaves anchoring their webs,

because I hate following orders, punching in and out,
because the interwoven blades—crossed swords

in a military wedding—drench me in the rising heat
and I drift along cramped paths sideways,

numbered rows, white tags at each end, unplugging
tassels with a pop, ripping out suckers and whips,

because a dog, a drenched black poodle—
out of place as I am, here in the plains

where the only myth is the way things are—
nips at my cuffs and tugs, like a devil reaching up,

and I leap back, startled,
on the matted tassels I've thrown to earth,

because the Pioneer Seed Company breeds hybrids,
and the sudden mud of a downpour

sucks my heels when thunder rumbles,
and I pull out tassels like pins from grenades,

because, when I yank one gone to seed,
a fine dust sifts, turning to grit on my sweaty arms,

and a thermos bottle swings from my belt,
and the fright-wigs of silk droop from swollen ears,

because the dry corn of late afternoon
rattles when the wind passes,

because, in the distance, a red hat bobs
as another man works alone.

The Biblical Garden

Naturally, it's plotted like a cross.
At the center, a worker lifts pots
of date palm and oleander
from a wheel barrow. Later he saws
a dead apricot—said to be the real
tree of knowledge—to a stump.

I latch the picket gate behind me,
warned against letting in the peacock
to rampage through mustard seeds,
still hearing trucks grind
on Cathedral Parkway, bottles smashed
in the new recycling center.

Sitting on a bench, I open up
a Bible once used on a ship—
with a name on the death page
and coordinates where they lowered his body
in the North Pacific—and locate
the verses listed on plaques.

At the far end, a goldfish pond
doubles for the Nile. Papyrus
clusters in the water, reeds on the bank
stiffen. As it points out in Kings,
if you leaned on a stalk
it would pierce you, like misplaced trust.

I look for "dove's dung,"
the Stars of Bethlehem, whose bulbs
were once ground for flour,
but the dirt patch is bare and raked.
I hear the squeals
of day campers racing in the parking lot.

I hear the cedars of Lebanon
brush against the cathedral wall,
the clicking sound
of squirrels as they dig near the roots,
a peacock's cry
and the squawking of chickens.

There's a hint of pink
in the weeds below where I'm sitting.
I reach down to retrieve
a flimsy letter, postmarked in Thailand,
slip it out and unfold
the goodbyes and excuses from a lover in the Peace Corps.

I think of the woman who read it
and tucked it away, under the stone bench,
looking, perhaps, at the flax
that exploded in a blue cloud,
angered by the sight
of the Judas tree in blossom.

Love, perhaps, led someone to clip
the Madonna lilies, leaving a bed of cut stems,
shunning the narcissus, the "rose"
for which the desert rejoiced—
flattened by cloudbursts, wilted by the heat.
A crowd has gathered. A guide clears her throat.

She explains how cumin and dill were used
to pay taxes, how judges carried
sprigs of rue into courtrooms because of the stench,
how olives were grown for lamp oil
since candles arose in the Middle Ages,
how Russians, on Palm Sunday, clutch pussy willows.

A faith in living things,
their flourishing, could grow here,
along the paths of cracked earth, where bees land
on the purple flowers of the hyssop,
where aloe leaves, rubbed on burns, are soothing,
where cinnamon leaves reek of camphor.

To whom can these blessings speak?
The bitter herbs and tamarisks
are so full of themselves, so complete,
they spring from the tended earth
of testaments, emerging like the willow to say
"I cover you with shadow, I compass you about."

To my mother, who taught me in Sunday School,
who gardened so aimlessly
her tomatoes, once halved,
had zinnia seeds inside,
the rye says, "I was not smitten
because I was not grown up."

To the kids on the blacktop
struggling at volleyball,
goaded by coaches who shout
Rotate! Serve! and blow whistles,
the bay tree says, "I spread
like the wicked in great power."

To the woman who wept
when she folded her letter
and slipped it in the envelope and hid it,
the mustard says, "I am the least
of seeds, but the birds of the air
will lodge in my branches."

Lanterns in the Trees

> I opened my eyes, everybody was looking up
> and pointing at Coco on the glacis railings with
> his feathers alight.
> —Jean Rhys, *Wide Sargasso Sea*

A clipped-winged parrot in a fire:
bad luck to see it die. *Bad luck,*
the janitor's ex-wife, wide-eyed from bourbon,
slurred, the pages of a thick book

parted beneath her fingers, like hair
checked for ticks. A monstrous volume
with pentagrams and wheels
and a text we took for voodoo.

Clapping it shut, she smoothed
her nurse's uniform and offered us the book—
Just for safe-keeping, just for luck.
We wanted her to keep

the spells and secrets to herself
in her cramped walk-up, lit by an aquarium,
with a striped Siamese and a band-aid tin
of relics—curls and fingernails.

A few weeks later, the local news
aired footage of her gutted flat,
the unexplainable blaze
"under investigation"—a brick facade

torched like a hive, the poverty
of a chest's missing drawer.
She tried to save her cat
by throwing him out her fifth-story window.

The magic book burned with her.
Despite our tingle of dread, she was right:
the book's dark alphabet
wouldn't have risen to suck our blood.

Mysteries are hidden best
in plain sight, a letter disguised
as a letter, a clue
too visible to seem mysterious—

as pirates in Barbados hung up
lanterns in the coconut trees
on the rocky coast. Incoming ships,
taking the blur of lights for Bridgetown,

crashed on the rocks
in a blaze of candles and shattered
surf and spars—plunder
in what might have been a haven.

Bad luck to come upon it—like a parrot,
poor phoenix, who can only say
Who's there? Who's there? on the railing
through flames, replying *I am. I am.*

EMBASSY ROW

The boy, in his basement room,
a wall safe hidden in the paneling,
lets in the stray cat
and almost falls asleep, shuddering
at the rise of women's voices
and a glass detonating in the sink.

Hardly able to stand it, he curls
around the snoozing cat and listens to the volleying,
not words but innuendo, a two-part invention
that grinds like a disposal
gnashing at the rush of water.

Against himself, he touches the floor tiles
with bare feet, climbs the staircase,
pushes the battered door that has no lock
and investigates the cold, enormous,
rented house on embassy row.

Two women. One sits in a puddle
of slick lily pads—her records,
her fragile 78s—weeping as she lifts them,
one by one, and shatters them on the floor.
The other scowls in the kitchen,
painting her nails, a highball on the tablecloth.

How often does this recur? In memory
it is nightly, permanent, like the wailer's claim
that the sulker held a blade to her spine
till early morning. But where, if true,
was the mound of wreckage, all that broken music?

And how did the boy slip back to his room,
down the warped stairs, and where was the cat,
and how could the moon squeeze itself
through a window sunk in a well of leaves,
and how could the noise die out,
as it did, in the cool air of this bunker?

The Dry Goods Store

for my mother

She made up games in the loft
above material racks, above a tape measure
hung on a nail. When her father smoothed a bolt,
she peeked through railings:

a roll of silk, long as the wake
of dredging boats on the solitary river.
Flat on the loft's high wharf
she counted up the barges piled

with organdy and taffeta,
gingham, calico, worsted, crepe.
Multiplied in mirrors, watched
by a headless lady, the metal dummy,

her father squeezed a bulb
that shot out chalk, marking the hem
with a crooked dotted line.
Overhead, the slow fan groaned.

A jar of dollars
wobbled along a cable through the store.
The lid unscrewed, he pinched
and twisted out the money.

Bills rustled in the cash drawer, bells
rang lightly as the door pane shuddered.
Her father returned to work
before the customers vanished, before the bells.

They must have thought him—what?
And what did she think, doting on thin hair
that bobbed below her, watching him measure cloth
and cut material with a wincing blade?

If she fell, her reflection would rise
through wood, the watery planks
she pretended she could dive in.
If she tore her frock, would he mend it?

Would he shake her? Would he cradle her,
in his woolen arms, to sleep?
Lips pinned, he turned below her,
dressing a mannequin behind closed drapes.

Soprano

for Carolyn Long

Can you still believe it—your flowery gowns,
a steamer trunk of glossies, press kits, raves from
    long-gone daily rags,
cameras popping when you swaggered off the Pullman
    car at dawn?
Can you believe the stir before the burial at sea?
When a steward knocked on the state room door,
you and the captain, buck naked, clinked tumblers in
    his rumpled bunk,
a funeral wreath haloed in your ringlets.

No one believes your stories, but all are true:
trimming the pompadour of Mario Lanza, presenting a
    baton—
Ormandy's gift when you dubbed in a part—to a patient
    who conducted to a record,
dancing in the White House, where the Vice President
    pinched your rear.
When a prop conked out on the airplane, ice on the
    wings over Wyoming,
you led the passengers in singing, insisting on four-part
    harmony.
Once down through the blizzard, you breezed on stage
    with your luggage,
flung your fur coat on the Steinway, and began an
    Italian air.

Little remains—your life on the road long over
and you back in Maryland, the tidewater inlets where
    your father tonged for oysters—

but nothing lets you go. You pencil on eyebrows, you
	pencil a blurry line
on the vodka bottle—someone's been cutting it with water.
Nothing can be trusted: your arteries mined,
your broken back still not knitting, your bones dissolving.
You press your hands on the hallway walls and edge
toward the toilet, but your feet lag behind, as if stuck.
You collapse, enormous, still muscle-bound from singing.

When you hacked through the Yucatan, digging out
	chiggers
and jotting down Mayan folk tunes, what were you after?
When you married a Marine who stormed Iwo Jima,
who captured a flag with a rising sun, whose letters were
	full of volcanic ash—
then dropped him for a cowboy, punching cattle on the
	ranges of Cuba,
what in the world were you after?
A lover who shot himself, a patron who left you stranded
	in Milan,
a tenor whose cock flopped out when he swooned on stage:
your laughter was taken for weeping, your greatest
	performance.

Pieces, nothing but pieces—a crossword puzzle
you're too bored to finish. Nothing matters, nothing
is ever worth a damn, can you believe no more than that?
If so, you're ready to believe anything:
the truth of commercials, the testimony of headlines—
"Top Docs Predict: Scientific Proof of an Afterlife."

In the life before, in Barcelona,
dust from the curtain almost choked you when it rose,
but you went on anyway—*Remember me, but ah,
  forget my fate.*
Now, you take it personally. What can I say
that won't hurt your feelings, since everything hurts,
a brusque reminder, and silence is unbearable
as the songs you hate to hear,
preferring talk shows on the radio as you sleep?
Cover your ears—and it just gets louder.
Open your mouth—and the world is all ovation, all
  applause.
Whether you like it or not, it makes you sing.

STORM ON FISHING BAY

What's hard to explain
darkens the prospect of happiness—
like wind picking up off shore
where four people retreat separately.

Darkened, the prospect of happiness
falls back to a hunting lodge
where four people retreat, separately
latching shutters, brewing coffee, gazing.

Fall's back. In a hunting lodge,
who is stirring the dust—
latching shutters, brewing coffee, gazing
at pictures spilled from an album?

Who is not stirring the dust?
The mother fussing? The boy who ponders
pictures spilled from an album?
The father quiet? The beautiful stranger singing?

The mother fusses at her boy, who ponders
what's hard to explain:
the father quiet, the beautiful stranger singing
like wind picking up off shore.

SIDE PANELS: ADAM AND EVE

1. After Cranach

They don't know what to call each other.
Crooking a finger, she slants her eyes
under arched eyebrows to where he stands,
bowlegged, scratching his head. He knows
that something is up: he wants the fruit
in her hand, though her whole body holds
the curve of harvests, and her breasts, round
as the globe in her palm, are softer,
more delicately tinged with russet.
He knows her hair, done up with gold leaf,
coils as serpentine as the dusty
coil in the branches. He wants to know
exactly what she wants in return.

2. After Dürer

Divided by their own perfection,
they are about to invent language,
their lips half parted, their bright eyes trained
past each other, their hands raised to grasp
what's beyond them now. They are about
to invent lies. All the milder eyes
of animals are upon them, on
their poised, hairless flesh, on the verge of
naming everything that touches them.
What brings them closer is their distance
and the sudden jet of gutturals,
aspirates, nasals, fricatives—all,
except the sibilance in the leaves,
knowledge in their own mouths. Flame to flame,
how else could they speak in tongues? How else
could glossaries come but by desire?

Learning Cursive

Slow in school, I needed tutoring
when Second Grade mastered script. So Terry Wright,
my classmate, opened her book-bag and peeled
    a sheet of paper from a pad,
holding her hand over mine as the pencil
glided from letter to letter, looping like a flying ace.
"Don't let your hand stop moving," Terry said.

The trick was how to keep connecting,
so we took turns peeling off each other's clothes
and running our fingers over curves and limbs,
    stripping to practice anywhere—
nude in my attic room; in a half-built tract house;
in a canvas hammock, where we fooled
with the plugs and sockets of a toy switchboard.

    And every meeting was a lesson—
Hold the pencil this way. Stroke like that.
    In dim rooms, she instructed me
how letters link, how bodies might connect
    like cut-outs, tab to slit.
On her blackboard, with the alphabet on top
    in white on green, we scrawled
    chalk outlines of genitals
and wiped them off with powdery erasers.
Naked beside a window, our bodies
were blank pages. Laughing, she told me "Here's
    how you touch me down there.
    Here's how you draw an *r*."

POSTMODERN LOVE

> . . . that faint thin line upon the shore!
> —George Meredith

Bright fuses, crackling as the surf ripped in,
dynamited along Long Island Sound
where we walked barefoot, cuffs rolled, hand in hand,
watching the die-hard waves, the demolition.
We drove there from our rented basement room
off a garage, where Russian wolfhound pups
cavorted, smearing the whole floor with their crap.
No wonder we feared both leaving and coming home,
slipping past, when the elegant borzois rutted.
The two of us? Entangled and glistening,
she came, once, with a surge, a charge. The thing
that made her moan, she later on admitted,
was thinking of a woman, a dirty blonde
she met for lunch but never dared to touch.
And that was love's high-tide mark at the beach:
a line of seaweed, broken shells, black sand.

PUBLICATION OF THE BRIDE SHEETS

After the wedding—
      in Mineola courthouse—
After the public service
      we had such trouble
finding the place
      and as we stood there
After the judge, a woman,
      handed us two booklets
with tassels, and we found
      the car with a parking ticket
I was moved, yes, but I knew
      I was making a mistake
We drove straight out
      to the tip of Long Island:
Montauk Point, with its broad-banded
      lighthouse and white concession stand.
The whole way there
      I said nothing,
or practically nothing.
      The whole way there.
In the dark we pulled off
      the sandy highway
onto sand, a rutted path,
      trying to reach the ocean,
but our heavy convertible
      ground to its axles,
catching on the roots
      but no that wasn't the time—
don't you remember?
      and we stacked up books

   and our oriental rug
      from the car's trunk
  under the tires, then revved up
      in reverse, but the tires
  kicked out the books,
      broke their spines, and unwound
  the Kurdistan rug. I chopped
      at the roots, all fibery
  and fraying like rope.
      We always took drives.
Anywhere. It didn't matter
      how far we reached, so long
as we got away:
      the quarter horse track
that went bankrupt later,
      the bottomless lake,
duck farms at the Moriches
      with their muddy birds
dragging clipped wings.
      Just before dawn
  the police came, called in
      an all-night tow truck
  that pulled us free.
      But we hadn't slept at all,
  huddled on bucket seats,
      bumping the gear stick,
  and couldn't sleep
      until the next day on the beach.
I slept in the sun.
      Later on, my face

turned wooden and charred,
        my eyes swelled up so much
they looked like the eyes
        of a subway poster girl, slit
and slashed lengthwise.
        In a city, far away,
as we walked from a movie,
        a grizzled unshaven tramp
turned suddenly, dangled
        a rat in her face.
She screamed. The couples
        under a café's umbrellas
laughed: they knew
        he'd been there for years,
at the same corner, maybe
        with the same dead rat.
It looked as if he shook
        a severed penis.
A block later, as I caught
        my breath, we heard
distant screams behind us, oddly
        like muffled church bells.
The judge said: just because
        this isn't a church,
with an organ and stained glass,
        it shouldn't be less special.
I pinned a flower,
        one her mother bought,
an orchid, on her blouse.
        And it smelled like nothing—

only the ashtray
>*on the judge's desk.*

Maybe, if we hadn't
>slept on bare springs,

if she hadn't been allergic
>to our second-hand mattress . . .

At dawn, when I came home
>*from waitressing, I needed you.*

Half-asleep, you still loved me
>*though I smelled like the smoke*

and grease of the diner.
>*It was in my hair*

and it covered you
>*and you didn't mind.*

If we hadn't tossed
>our rings in the river,

maybe, if we went back . . .
>*On the shoulder, hitch-hikers*

waited, waved, and we passed by.
>*No one could join us.*

Maybe, if another . . .
>*No one could change us.*

If we kept on driving,
>perpetual tourists,

if we kept on looking . . .
>*If we kept on looking*

at the road itself:
>*the foliage, brown*

from headlights and exhaust,
>*and the spattered animals*

like warnings, and the signs
 flashing when the wind blew,
and the sand across asphalt—
 the endless road, ending.

John Drury is the author of *Creating Poetry, The Poetry Dictionary,* and a chapbook of poems, *The Stray Ghost.* His work has appeared in *Poetry, Shenandoah, The Paris Review, The New Republic, The American Poetry Review, The Southern Review, The Hudson Review, Western Humanities Review,* and a *Pushcart Prize* anthology. He was born in Cambridge, Maryland, and now lives in Cincinnati with his wife, Laurie Henry, and their two children, Eric and Rebecca. He teaches at the University of Cincinnati.